WORKING OUT WITHOUT WEIGHTS

WORKING OUT

By CHUCK GAYLORD
Featuring MITCH GAYLORD

Photographs by Mark Hanauer

William Morrow and Company, Inc. / New York

WITHOUT WEIGHTS

Library of Congress Cataloging in Publication Data

Gaylord, Chuck.
    Working out without weights.

    Includes index.
    1. Exercise.   2. Gymnastics.   1. Hanauer, Mark.
II. Title.
GV481.G39   1985   796.4'1   84-29606
ISBN 0-688-04811-0

Printed in the United States of America

First Edition

1 2 3 4 5 6 7 8 9 10

BOOK DESIGN BY LINEY LI

For Dean Pitchford, *who made this book possible*

ACKNOWLEDGMENTS

For their help with this book, thanks to Kevin Supple, Art Shurlock, my family, my agent, Luis Sanjurjo, and my editor, Doug Stumpf.

INTRODUCTION

The Joy of Gymnastics and Gymnastics Exercises

Anyone who has ever seen a gymnastics meet knows that few sports are more exciting to watch. Any gymnast knows there is no sport more exciting to participate in.

What are the rewards of being a gymnast? The feeling of exhilaration as you fly through the air, stretching the capacities of human movement and coordination to almost superhuman limits. The feeling of accomplishment when, after long hours of practice and concentration, you develop the skill and confidence to perform a new move that few other people can do. The sense of well-being you get from knowing that your body is totally efficient—strong, with no extra bulk, and able to move freely. Gymnasts can never resist the urge to play, and as a result, I think they stay young longer.

During the decade or so that I've been involved with gymnastics, the sport has evolved so rapidly that it's difficult to believe. It first gained wide, popular appeal when two Eastern European charmers—Olga Korbut at the 1972 Olympics and Nadia Comaneci in 1976—fired the public's imagination with their disarming youth, wonderfully graceful moves, and incredible discipline. In America, men's gymnastics has truly come into its own during the last year—as a result of the gold-medal-winning American men's team at the 1984 Olympics in Los Angeles.

The sport has changed not only with regard to public recognition, but internally as well. As short a time as five years ago, in any given routine a gymnast would include only one really difficult move. Today, it's not unusual to see five or six difficult moves per routine. In fact so many perfect 10 scores were awarded at the 1984 Olympics that it appears the sport has outgrown its scoring system. Many people now think the scoring system should be revised accordingly.

All of this seems to indicate that we have entered a "golden age" of gymnastics. Gymnastics clubs are springing up across the country, and school gymnastics teams are being put on an equal footing with those of more traditional sports, such as baseball or football. People are more familiar with gymnastics terms and moves, and the sport's leading practitioners are now recognized as celebrities.

The purpose of this book is not to turn you into a competitive gymnast. To do that would take years of dedication and practice on your part and could be accomplished only under the close personal supervision of a good coach who knows what he's doing. In addition, gymnastics as a competitive sport is exclusively for the young—whose bodies are at their most agile and flexible.

Nor is this book a basic course in gymnastics.

Working Out Without Weights is, as the title implies, a fitness system based on the principles of gymnastics. These days, Americans are more concerned than ever about becoming and staying fit. The advantages of having a healthy, trim, attractive body are so obvious that they don't need to be enumerated here.

The exercises contained in this book are the same ones that gymnasts use to attain their phenomenal strength and flexibility, their muscular, well-proportioned, and graceful bodies. For reasons I'll go into a little later, I feel that this system is superior to any other you can adopt. If you learn and regularly practice these exercises, you'll be amazed at the changes in how you look and feel. That healthy, muscular, well-proportioned, and graceful body is yours for the asking! As a bonus you'll come to understand a little better what the sport of gymnastics is all about and how it's done.

The Genesis of This Program, and Why You Should Use It

My brother and I started doing gymnastics together in high school. At that time we both were too small for such conventional sports as football or basketball and although later we both grew to average height, we enjoyed gymnastics too much to consider switching to another sport.

I went on to the University of California, Davis, with the idea of becoming a veterinarian. I joined the gymnastics team there and eventually became a nine-time collegiate all-American. Meanwhile Mitch went to UCLA and joined its gymnastics team. For a brief time we competed in the same international meets. While in college, I took some teaching jobs on the side, working with a girls' competitive gymnastics club, and setting up a gymnastics program at a local air force base. I discovered that coaching was something I enjoyed doing. After graduation, I joined a professional cross-country gymnastics tour. When it ended in 1982, Mitch asked me to coach him for the 1984 Olympics. The rest, as they say, is history.

During the two years I was coaching Mitch, I worked in movies to support myself (I was Kevin Bacon's gymnastics double in *Footloose*). Often dancers, actors, and other athletes would ask me to teach them gymnastics strength and flexibility exercises to help them improve their physiques and perform better in their jobs. I began to see that everyone could benefit from gymnastics exercises, not just gymnasts and people who were already athletes.

In 1983 I gave a class for nonathletes, mainly businesspeople in their thirties and forties who didn't get a chance to work out much. When we started, most people in the class could barely do one pull-up. After three months, all could do at least ten pull-ups and fifty push-ups. They could do handstands and even push-ups from a handstand position. All could claim improved flexibility and

Chuck Gaylord

range of motion. One class member, who ran regularly, noted that as a result of our class he carried himself better and enjoyed running more.

Best of all, members of the class felt healthier and thought they had substantially improved the strength and appearance of their bodies.

In this book you will find exactly the same routine that we used for our class. They're also the same exercises I used to train Mitch for the Olympics.

Gymnastics flexibility and strength exercises obviously get results. But why adopt them over other fitness systems?

Virtually every other fitness system that is currently popular emphasizes some form of weight training—either with free weights or on Universal, Nautilus, or other machines. When people see gymnasts' well-defined musculature, they assume we work out with weights. This is entirely false. I never knew a gymnast who employed weight training. We use gymnastics exercises instead, even when we need to build strength in a specific area.

As I see it, gymnastics exercises have several advantages over weight training. With gymnastics exercises you use your body rather than something external to it, building strength with movements natural to your body. Weight-training exercises tend to focus on one muscle or muscle group at a time, whereas gymnastics exercises work many muscles simultaneously and develop coordination.

Flexibility and ease of motion are an integral part of the gymnast's program. At best, weight lifters view stretching as a necessary evil and therefore tend to deemphasize or neglect it. For that reason, and because of the inherent dangers of lifting heavy weights (including the stress they place on the lower back), it's far easier to injure yourself lifting weights than it is doing gymnastics exercises.

But most important, I think gymnastics exercises are a more enjoyable way to stay in shape. You feel a true sense of accomplishment and adventure because learning the exercises is like learning a new trick or developing a new talent.

Even if you do decide that a weight-training program is for you, you should consider learning this program as a supplement. When you're traveling, it's not usually possible to take weights along, and some days you simply won't have time to go to the gym. Instead of doing nothing at all, you could be working out without weights.

Mitch Gaylord

The Gymnast's Body

Contemporary American society places a high value on physical fitness—and on the trim, attractive body that comes with it. Probably one of the main reasons you've decided to start working out is to develop a better body. If that's so, you couldn't have chosen a better method than this one.

Even among athletes, gymnasts have some of the most muscular, trim, and well-proportioned bodies going. I've never seen a fat gymnast, and the reason is simple. In order to accomplish the difficult moves of his sport, the gymnast's body must be totally efficient. There is simply no room for excess weight.

Most athletes work on their feet, but gymnasts spend a good deal of their time supporting their weight with their arms, shoulders, back, and chest. If you doubt this, just watch any routine on the rings, high bar, pommel horse, or parallel bars. Not surprisingly, the result is a highly developed upper body. But unlike weight lifters, whose muscles tend to bulk out to enormous size, gymnasts retain a neat, compact, *light* look. The emphasis is on quickness and agility, on muscle definition rather than muscle size.

Despite gymnastics' focus on upper-body strength, other parts of the body are not neglected. Strong abdominal muscles are crucial for controlling body position in gymnastics moves. And the legs must be able to withstand high-bar landings from as high as fifteen feet.

In the accompanying photos of Mitch, we've labeled some of the more important muscles. We will be referring to these throughout the book.

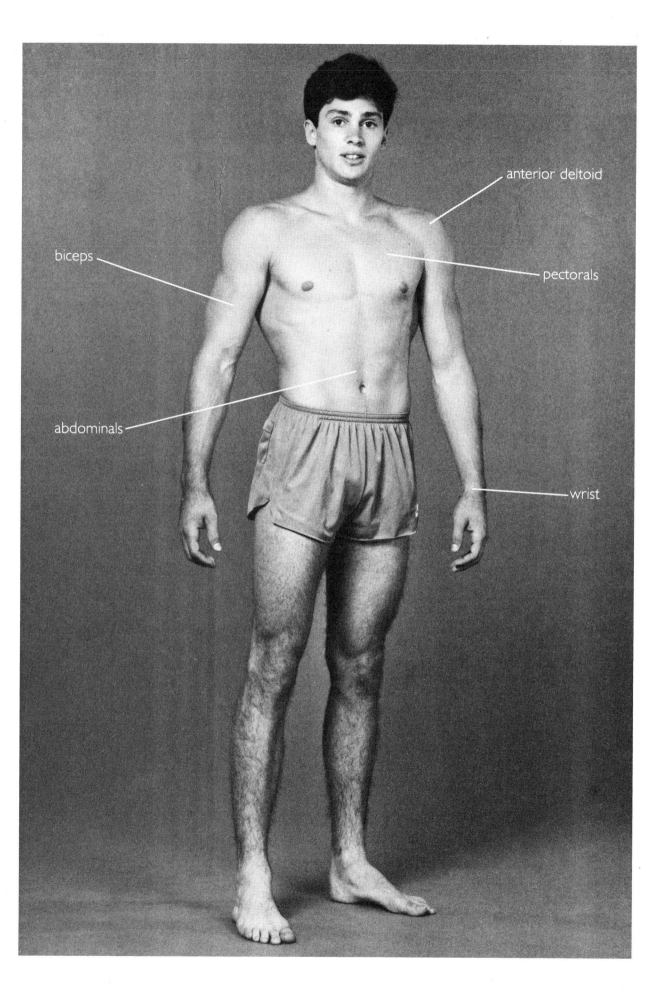

anterior deltoid

biceps

pectorals

abdominals

wrist

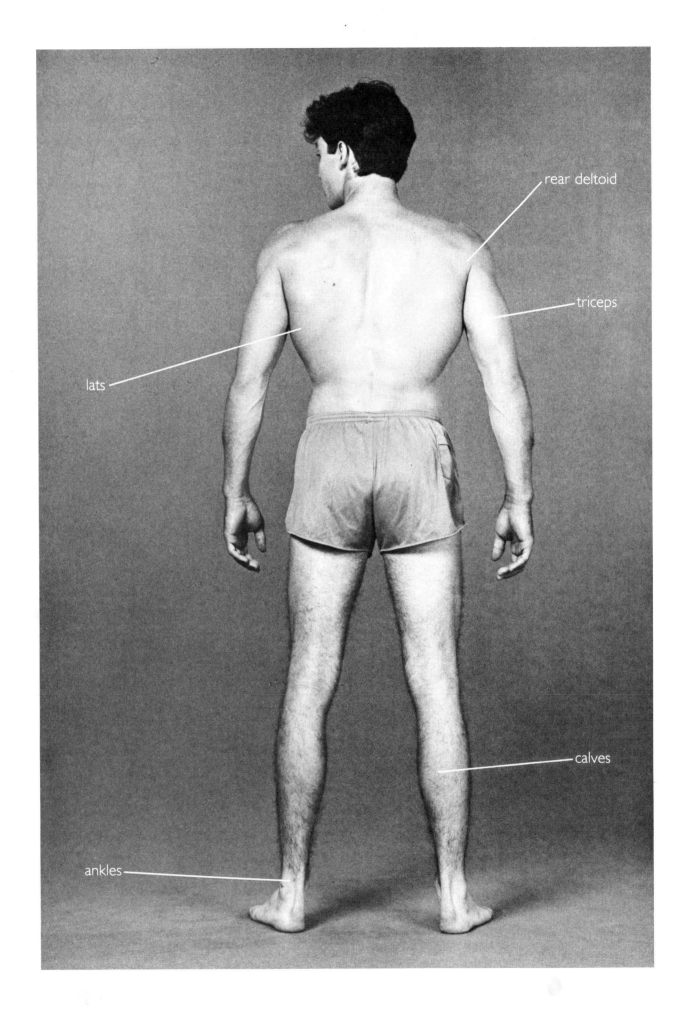

rear deltoid

triceps

lats

calves

ankles

The Program

This book is divided into three parts: a *basic exercise circuit, advanced exercises,* and *exercises for the gym.*

The basic circuit is an exercise program consisting of warm-ups, stretches, and strength-building exercises for the abdominal muscles, legs, and upper body (arms, shoulders, chest, and back). The purpose of the warm-ups is to get your blood moving and to get you in the mood for exercise. The stretches are flexibility exercises for your muscles, joints, tendons, and ligaments. Flexibility is emphasized heavily in this program—after all, gymnastics is defined by strength through a full range of motion. But stretching is *absolutely essential* before any exercise. It helps prevent injuries and makes your body movements more efficient. In addition, I suggest that you do some stretching immediately after finishing any workout, including our basic circuit. Not only will you be able to stretch farther then, you'll also counteract any muscle tightness acquired during exercise.

For each of the strength-building exercises I've given a starting-point number of repetitions, or "reps" (a repetition is one complete performance of an exercise movement—from the starting position, through the entire movement, and back to the starting position), and a goal toward which to work. As I stress throughout, the starting points are intended for a person already in relatively good shape. If you can't do that many repetitions, don't worry about it and don't give up. Do as many as you can (with proper technique, as described in each exercise) and use the starting point as your goal. On the other hand, if you are not challenged by the starting number of repetitions, don't be afraid to begin with more.

In the advanced exercise section, I've given you exercises to add when you can comfortably complete the basic circuit and need a greater challenge. With these more difficult exercises, you'll notice that you're doing some of the same movements that gymnasts use in their routines.

In the final section of the book, you'll find exercises to do if you have access to some gymnastics equipment. Many people belong to a gym these days, and most gymnasiums have at least a set of parallel bars.

What This Program Will Not Do

While this workout method can work wonders for you, you should not expect it to do things that it's not intended to do. For one thing, it's not a weight-loss program. There is one way, and only one way, to lose weight: Burn up more calories than you eat. In simple terms that means you have to eat less and/or burn up more calories through some vigorous activity like swimming, running, or bicycling. If you need to lose weight, you should consult a doctor about finding a method that's right for you.

While we're on the subject of diet, I should note that if you care enough about your body to adopt this exercise regimen, you should also care enough to eat right. Your muscles cannot perform to full capacity if they're not being properly nourished. A discourse on the subject is beyond the scope of this book, but you probably know the basics of good nutrition anyway. Let's just repeat here that you'll look, feel, and perform better if you cut down on things that are bad for you: alcohol, refined sugar, processed foods, and fats, and eat more of the things that are good for you: whole grains, fresh fruits and vegetables, complex carbohydrates.

Another thing the exercises in this book won't do is supply you with aerobic activity. Just as important as keeping your outer body in good shape is keeping your inner body fit, by which I mean exercising your cardiovascular system. It has recently been shown that regular aerobic exercise—such as running, swimming, bicycling, or aerobic dance—significantly decreases your chances of having a heart attack. In addition, aerobic activity burns up calories.

To reap the benefits of aerobic exercise you have to get your heart going at a pretty fast clip—about 60 to 80 percent of your maximum heart rate—for about half an hour. In practical terms that means you've got to pursue the aerobic activity of your choice with some enthusiasm, pushing yourself *slightly*. You should not push yourself so much that you feel pain or disabling fatigue; exercise should always be fun, not an ordeal. If you have any doubts, or if you have not exercised regularly for quite some time, you should consult a doctor and have a full checkup before you start. In the next section, I'll suggest ways of integrating aerobic activity into the exercises in this book.

THE BASIC CIRCUIT

The exercises in the basic circuit should take you about an hour to perform.

How many times a week should you do the circuit? That's really up to you, but I recommend the following schedule: Do the complete circuit three times a week, every other day—for example, on Monday, Wednesday, and Friday. On the days in between (Tuesday, Thursday, and Saturday), you should do the stretching and abdominal sections of the circuit only, and then follow them with at least half an hour of the aerobic activity of your choice. That leaves you one day of the week free.

When during the day should you do the circuit? If you're a morning person, do it first thing in the morning. Some businesspeople like to skip lunch and exercise during their lunch hours. It's really up to you. I think it is helpful to select the same time every day for exercise—that way you will make exercise an automatic part of your schedule, a habit. However, for people with busy and varied schedules, this is not always possible. The one time you probably won't want to exercise is directly after eating a big meal. Not only will you feel sluggish then, but your muscles are not going to be getting the energy they need; instead that energy's being used to help you digest the food.

Where should you do the exercises? I've designed this program so it can be performed at home. You'll need a space large enough so that you're not knocking things over or bumping into them. In addition, you should work on a mat, carpet, or other padded surface. *You should not exercise on a hardwood, tile, or other hard floor.*

We said on the cover that no special gymnastics equipment was required. We didn't want you to think you had to go out and buy a pommel horse to use this book. Actually one piece of special equipment is essential and another would be extremely useful. The first is a portable chinning bar, readily available at most sport-

Typical Workout Schedule

MON	TUES	WED	THURS	FRI	SAT	SUN
complete program	stretching & abdominals & aerobics	complete program	stretching & abdominals & aerobics	complete program	stretching & abdominals & aerobics	rest

ing goods stores. You can install it in any doorway in a few minutes.

The second piece of equipment, which is not absolutely necessary but which would be extremely useful, is a set of parallettes. These are a pair of handles that sit a few inches off the floor. They are used for doing push-ups and other exercises in which you support your weight with your hands—thus offering something to hold on to and adding a little height. In any exercise where parallettes can be used, I've first given directions for doing it without them. If you can get a pair, though, by all means do so. Most gymnasts have custom-made wooden parallettes (a picture of mine is below). If you're handy you can build your own pair, or perhaps you can get a carpenter or your local high-school woodshop to build you a pair. Most sporting goods stores carry a commercially made chrome version called Exer-Bars (also pictured opposite). They cost about thirty dollars. In addition, GSC Athletic Equipment sells a wooden and chrome version under the name

Wooden parallettes

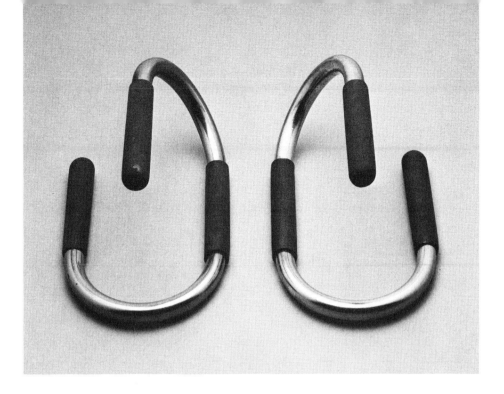

Commercially made chrome parallettes

"Hand Stand Pairoletts." They cost thirty-eight dollars and if your local sporting goods store doesn't have them, you can write directly to the manufacturer at 600 North Pacific Avenue, San Pedro, California 90733. One final word of advice here: I've noticed that most often sales clerks know parallettes by some other name—"push-up bars," for example—so be sure to describe what you want when you go to buy them.

For working out, you should, of course, wear athletic clothing—gym shorts or sweats are fine. The main thing to remember is that since you'll be moving and stretching into unorthodox positions, you won't want your clothes to be so tight as to be binding or so loose that they get in your way. Most of the exercises in the book should be performed barefoot or wearing socks only. The exceptions are the warm-up and leg exercises, for which you should wear running or tennis shoes.

For some of the exercises, I've suggested that a partner would be helpful, at least to start out. In certain flexibility exercises, a partner can help you stretch a little farther. For the handstand exercises, a partner can spot for you until you gain the skill and confidence to perform them alone. But in general, working out with a partner is recommended. It forces you to schedule (and keep) firm appointments to work out. It's also nice to have someone around to offer encouragement, to keep you from cheating, and generally to have fun with.

Once you're doing the exercises regularly, you'll begin to notice good things happening to your body. You'll feel more comfortable with everyday movements, even in stationary postures such as standing or sitting. As you grow stronger, the exercises will get easier and you'll enjoy doing them more. Your muscles will begin to bulge in an attractive way.

As I've already said, it's difficult to injure yourself doing these exercises—difficult but not impossible. Any time you move, you can pull a muscle. The stretching exercises in this program will minimize this possibility. However, avoid sudden, jerky movements while exercising and never bounce while stretching. If some part of your body is especially sensitive, or the victim of an old injury, be especially easy on it. For instance, if you have a weak lower back, be particularly careful doing exercises that place a strain on that area. If it actually hurts to do any exercise, stop doing it immediately. You must wait until the injured body part heals completely (it could take days or even weeks) before trying to exercise again. If pain persists, you should drop the exercise from your circuit altogether.

This is not to say that you won't feel some discomfort while exercising. Doing a simple push-up with correct technique can be difficult if you don't have the necessary strength. But there is a *big* difference between discomfort and pain. Get in touch with your body so that you know the difference.

So that's it! You're ready to start working out.

Warm-ups

To start out, let's get your body moving, your blood flowing, and your heart pumping a little faster. These exercises should work up a light sweat and get you in the mood for physical activity. Don't overexert yourself: The main object here is to stay loose. For this group of exercises (and later, for the leg exercises), you should wear sneakers.

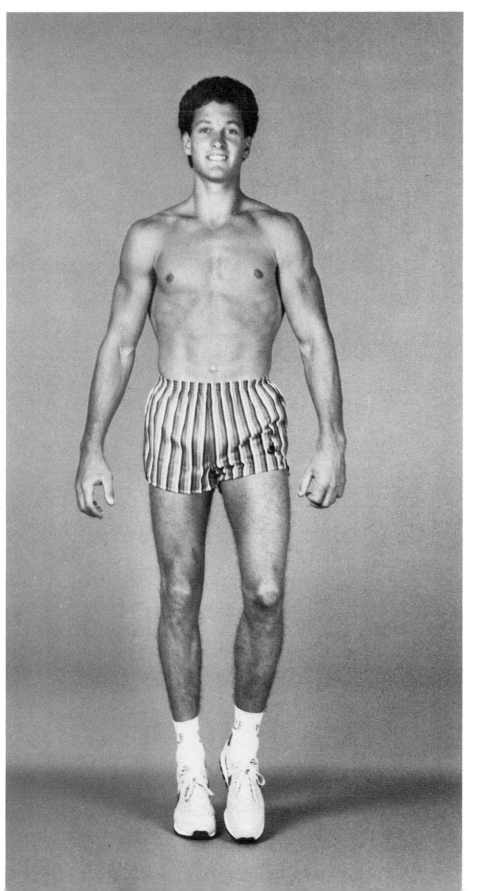

Letting your arms dangle loosely at your sides and keeping your whole body relaxed, lightly jog in place. But don't just jog—get up on your toes, and dance around a little, like a boxer.

J UMPING UP AND DOWN   **I minute**

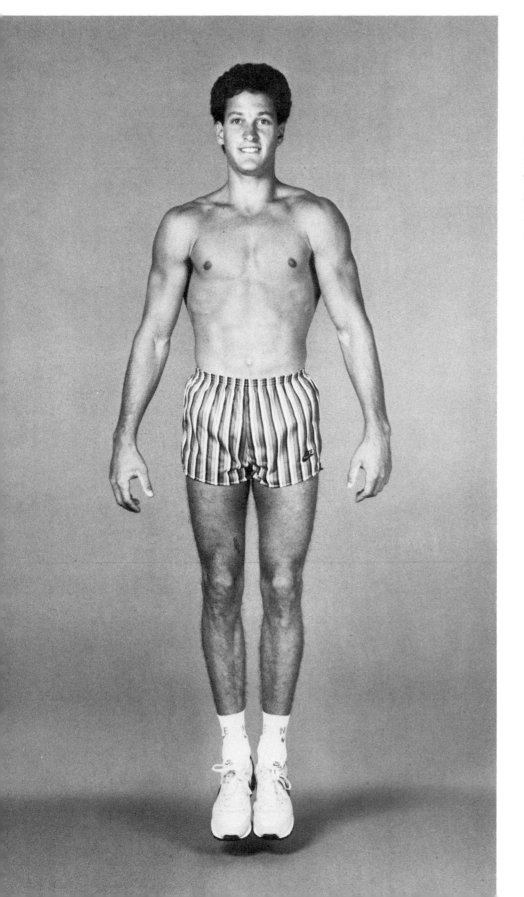

Hang your arms loosely at your sides again and put your feet together. Now jump straight up and down on the balls of your feet, rising an inch or two off the floor each time.

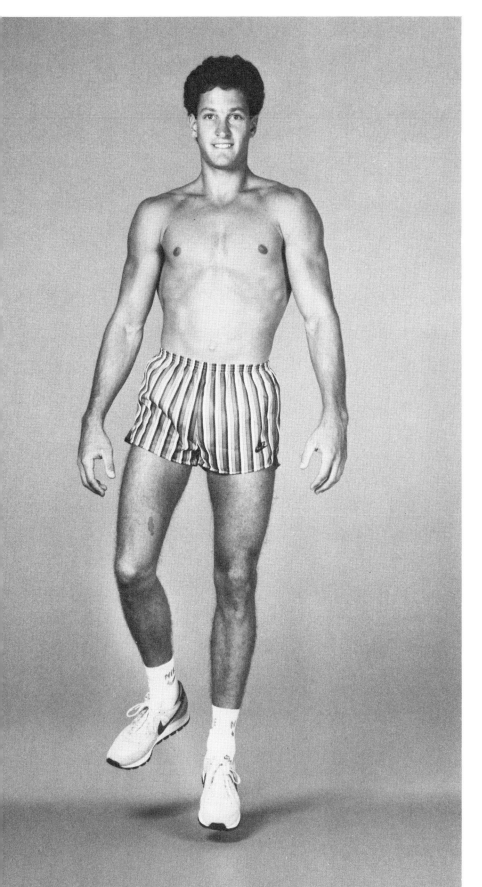

This is a light hop. Don't try to jump like Superman.

J UMPING JACKS   **1 minute**

But don't bring your arms up—just let them hang loosely at your sides.

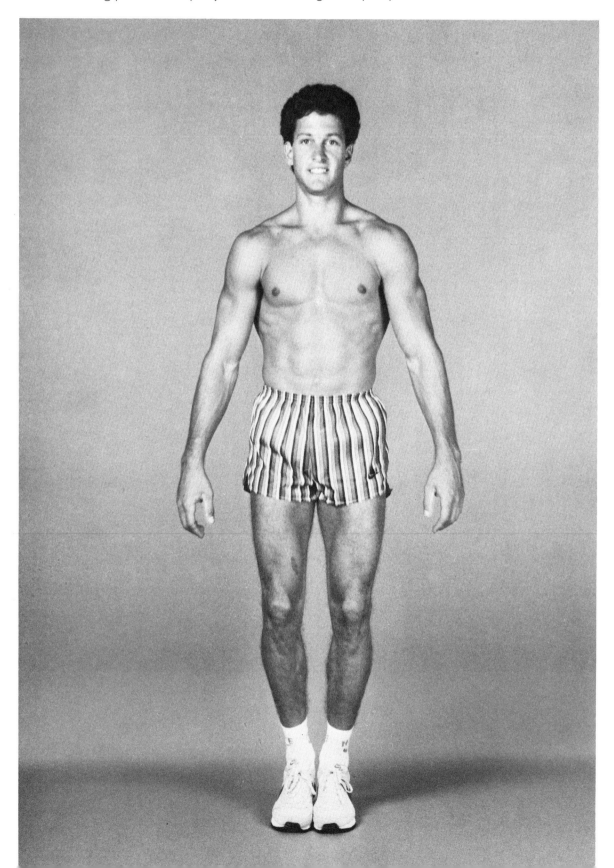

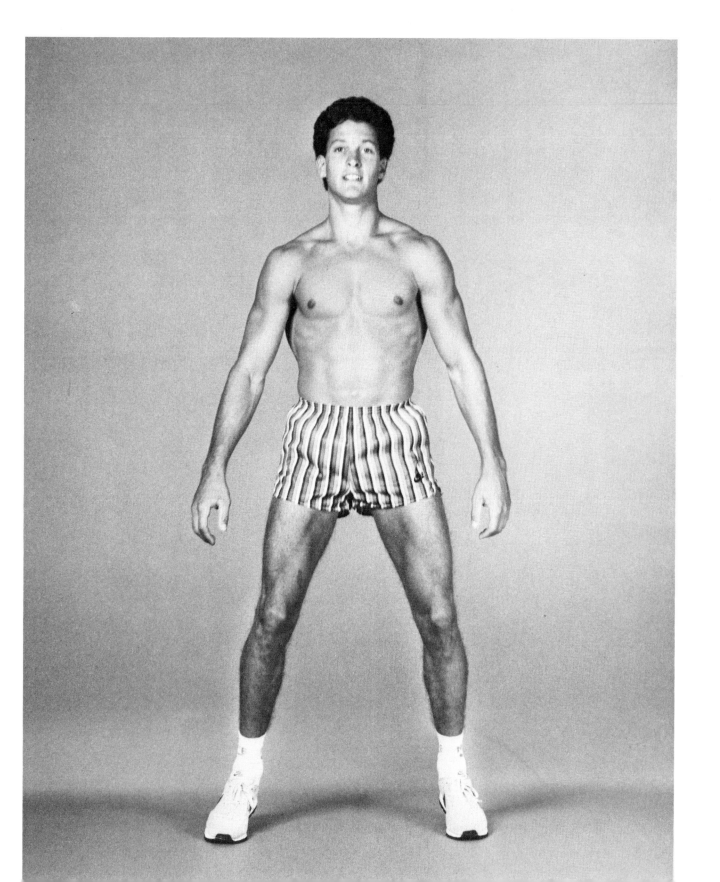

Put one foot twelve to eighteen inches behind the other. As you jump up, switch feet. Stay on your toes, continuing at a snappy pace.

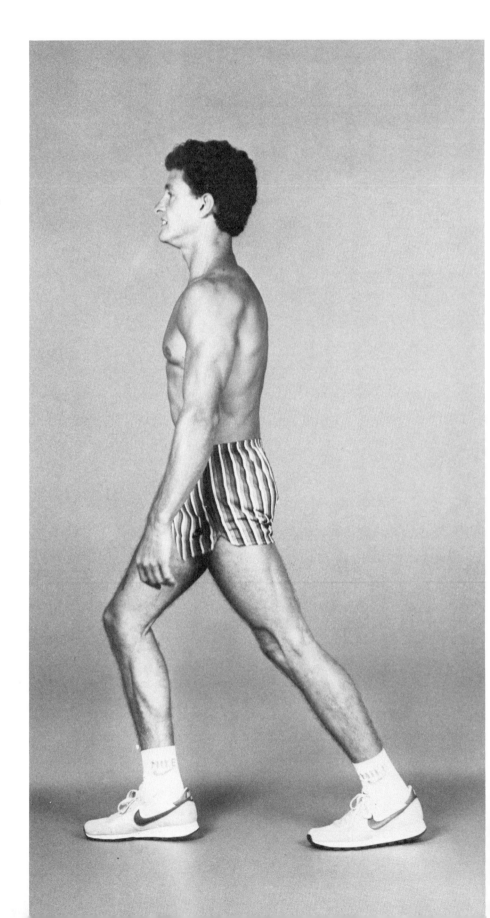

P UNCH JUMPS **30 seconds**

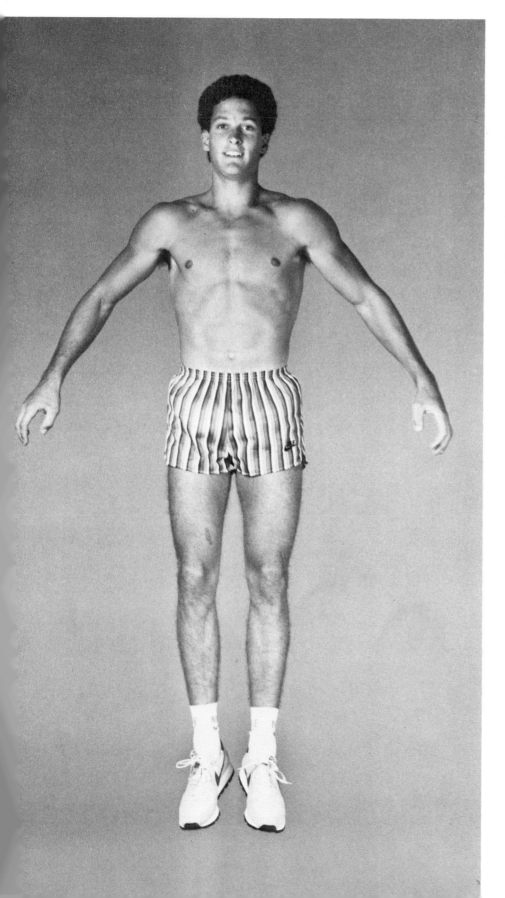

This exercise is the one exception in the group: Go all out. With feet together, jump quickly and powerfully as high as you can. Keep your legs tight and bend your knees only slightly each time you land. Stay on your toes and bounce when you hit the floor.

Mitch Gaylord performing a giant swing on the rings

Stretching

Most athletes don't bother to stretch properly, and as a result often get injured. For example, runners constantly complain of hamstring pulls. They should take a cue from gymnasts, who count flexibility as one of their chief concerns. Gymnastics movements—from a simple split in floor exercise to a giant swing on the rings—are not possible without a great degree of flexibility. And stretching not only prevents injuries and increases your range of motion—it also feels good.

The following exercises are meant to stretch out your muscles, tendons, ligaments, and joints before you go on to more strenuous exercise. They are the same movements gymnasts use to attain their tremendous flexibility.

Hold each stretching position in this section for at least twenty seconds. Don't bounce—that's more likely to pull your muscles than stretch them. Different people have different degrees of flexibility, so don't worry if you can't stretch as far as Mitch does in the photos; it took him many years to get to this point.

The important thing is to pay attention to what your body is telling you. Don't stretch so far that you feel actual pain; on the other hand, don't take it too easy on yourself—if you don't feel some discomfort, you're probably not doing very much.

Be patient. If you stretch regularly, you'll start noticing a gradual but definite improvement.

Stand in a relaxed position with your arms at your sides. Let your head fall to the left as far as it will go, keeping your neck and shoulders relaxed. Now circle your head slowly down to the front so that your chin is close to your chest. Continue circling slowly clockwise, over your right shoulder

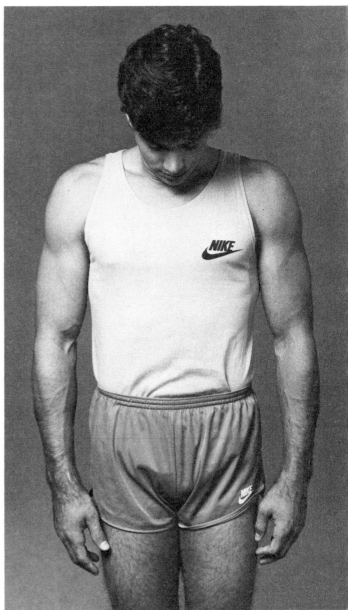

and then to the back so that your head is hanging back limply. Now finish the circle over your left shoulder and start down again. After five complete circles, reverse the direction of the rotation.

F ORWARD AND BACKWARD ARM CIRCLES

Starting with your arms straight over your head, palms facing forward, let them drop in front of you down to your sides, then circle back up behind you to the starting position. Keep your arms straight and as close together

as possible at the top of the circle. After ten repetitions, reverse the rotation and make backward circles.

CROSS-ARM SWINGS   *10 reps*

Extend your arms straight out to the sides at shoulder level. Swing them forward so that they cross in front of you, one arm above the other. Without stopping, swing them back as far as they'll go, then forward again so that the bottom arm is on top and the top arm is on bottom. Keep your arms straight, but not locked, throughout.

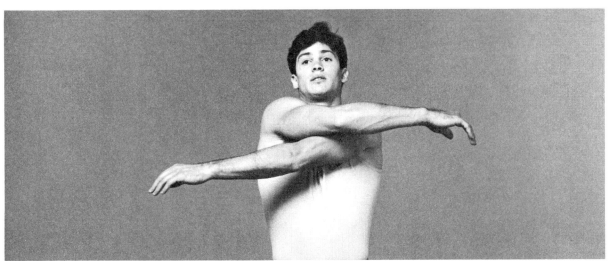

V ERTICAL ARM SWINGS   **10 reps**

Starting with your arms straight above your head, palms facing forward, swing your arms forward and down past your sides and as far back as possible, then instantly back up in front of you to the starting position. Again, keep your arms straight, but not locked.

T RUNK TWISTERS **10 reps**

Stand with your feet slightly farther apart than shoulder width. Extend your arms straight out in front of you at shoulder level. Swing them to the left and then, without stopping, to the right. Let your shoulders and upper body twist as far as possible in each direction, but don't let your feet move. This is a great stretch for your waist and lower back.

Again your feet should be slightly farther apart than shoulder width. Place your left hand on your left hip and raise your right hand over your head. Bend to the left and stretch over your left hip, without bending forward at the waist. Let your left arm slide down your left leg and use this arm for support. Hold a good stretch, then switch sides.

TRUNK CIRCLES *5 circles each direction*

With feet a little farther apart than shoulder width, stand with your hands on your hips. Let your upper body fall forward, bending at the waist, then circle your entire torso up over your right side. Continue the circle until your head and shoulders are as far back behind your hips as possible, then

circle down over your left side and finish in the starting position. Reverse directions after five complete circles. You should feel stretches in your sides, hips, stomach, and hamstrings.

 # RIST STRETCHES   **Hold each position 20 seconds**

From a kneeling position:

a) Place your palms flat on the floor, fingers facing forward, about two inches in front of your knees. Keep your arms straight and gently lean out over your hands.

b) Place your palms flat on the floor, fingers facing backward and gently lean back away from your hands.

c) Place the backs of your hands on the floor, fingers facing forward, and gently lean over your hands.

d) Place the backs of your hands on the floor, fingers facing backward and gently lean back away from your hands.

e) Place your palms flat on the floor, directly next to your knees, fingers facing outward. For 20 seconds rock from side to side over each wrist.

After you finish all five stretches, shake your wrists out. These exercises prepare you for the many moves coming up in which you will be supporting your weight with your hands (push-ups, for example).

CALF AND ACHILLES TENDON STRETCHES

Hold each position at least 20 seconds

Get down on all fours, then straighten your legs and push your weight back onto the balls of your feet, so that your hips are high off the floor.

Position one: Press your heels toward the floor and hold so that you feel the stretch in your calves.

Position two: Now bend your knees slightly toward the floor to feel the stretch more in your Achilles tendons.

HAMSTRING STRETCH A **Hold at least 20 seconds each leg**

Sitting on the floor, with your left leg straight out in front of you, bend your right leg so that the sole of your right foot is resting against the inner thigh of your left leg and your right knee is on or close to the floor. Extend your arms as far down your left leg as possible. Grab hold and pull

your upper body down, trying not to bend your left leg. Then switch legs and repeat.

You may want to use a partner to help on this exercise. Have him stand behind you and apply *gentle* pressure to your lower back to help you stretch farther down the leg.

52   With feet flexed

Sitting with your legs together and straight out in front of you, reach as far down your legs as possible, grab hold, and pull your upper body down, making sure to bend from the waist. Do this stretch first with toes pointed, then with feet flexed back.

Once again you can use a partner to help you get farther down your legs.

With partner

S TRADDLE STRETCH   **Hold at least 20 seconds each position**

Sitting on the floor with your legs straight and spread as far apart as possible:

a) Extend your arms and reach as far down your left leg as you can. Grab hold and pull your upper body down.

b) Repeat over your right leg.

c) Reach down your right leg with your right hand and your left leg with your left hand. Grab hold as far down each leg as you can and pull your upper body down into the middle of the straddle.

Remember not to bend at the knees. Bend at the waist, and try to keep your weight evenly distributed on both buttocks. This is another exercise in which a partner can be extremely helpful by applying gentle pressure to your lower back.

Make sure your partner doesn't push too hard!

I NNER-THIGH STRETCH   **Hold at least 20 seconds**

Sit on the floor with the soles of your feet together, pulled in as close as possible. Grab hold of your toes with both hands, and if your knees are not already on the floor, use your elbows to push them down toward the floor. At the same time pull your upper body down toward your toes.

Sit with your legs straight out in front of you and place your hands behind your hips, palms flat on the floor and fingers facing backward. Slide your hips forward, so that you are sitting as far away from your hands as possible. Now bring your knees up until your feet are resting flat on the floor. Rock your knees from side to side, feeling the stretch in your shoulders.

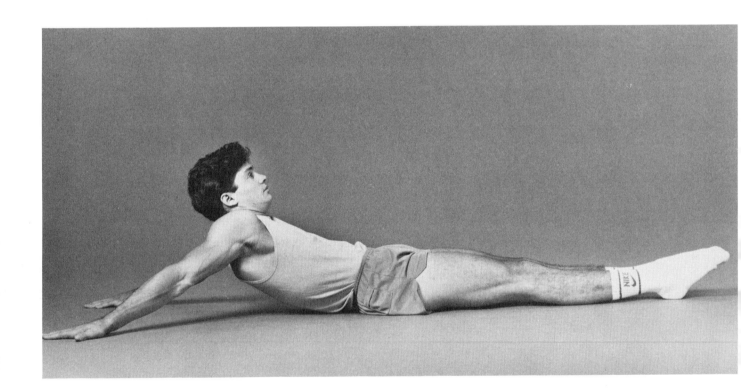

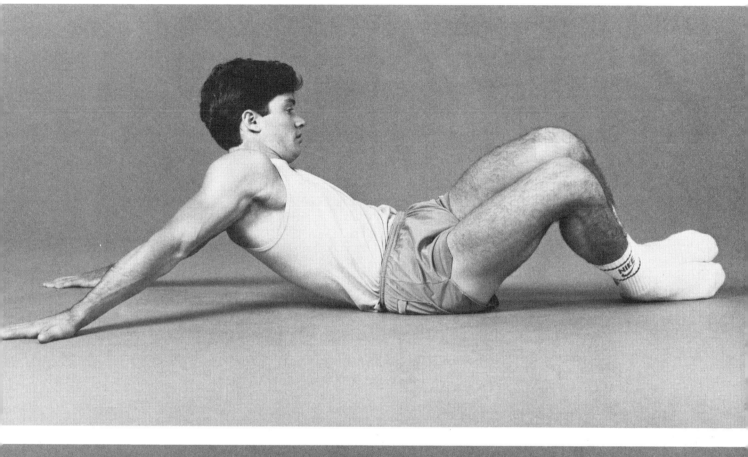

S TOMACH AND LOWER-BACK STRETCH   **Hold at least 20 seconds**

Lie on your stomach, placing your hands directly under or slightly in front of your shoulders, palms flat on the floor. Then push your shoulders and chest off the floor by straightening your arms, but try to keep your hips close to the floor.

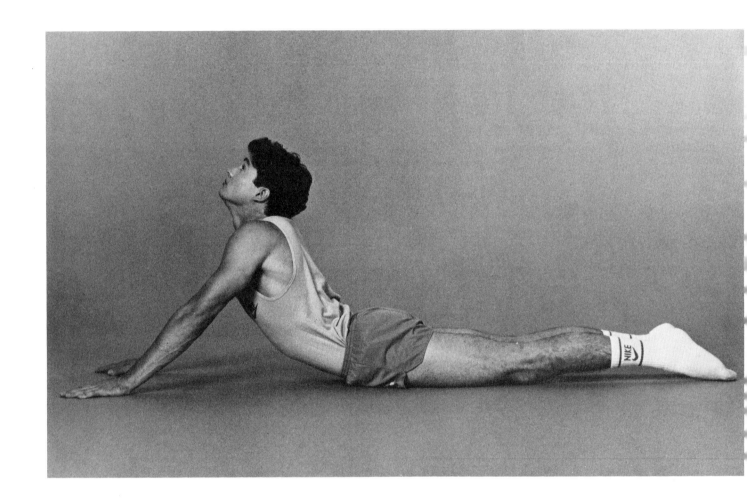

B | ACK BEND   **Hold at least 20 seconds**

Lying on your back, place your palms flat on the floor next to your ears, fingers pointing toward your feet. Pull your knees up so that your feet are flat on the floor, as close to your buttocks as possible. Push up so that your back arches and your arms and legs straighten out. You should look at the floor between your hands. Try to get your hands and feet close together, and push yourself up as high as possible, onto your toes if you c

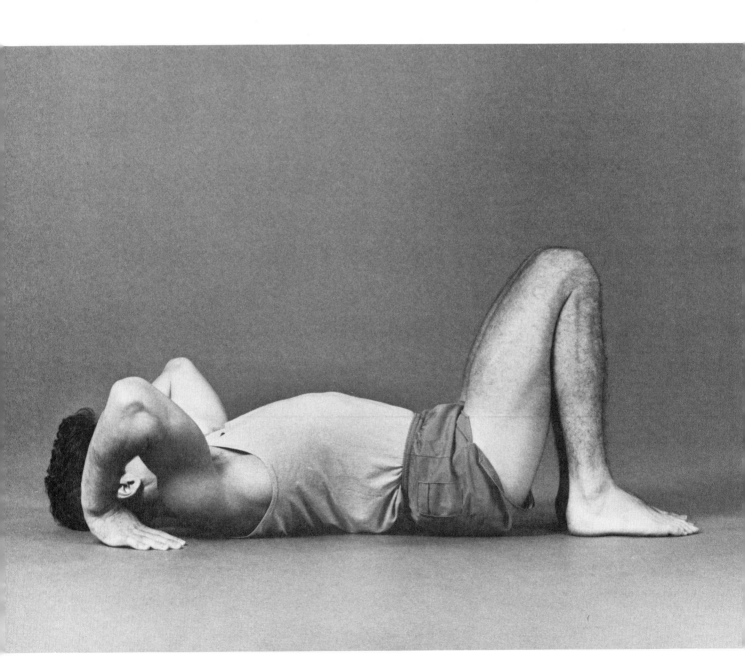

This is a particularly good exercise because it stretches your hips, stomach, upper and lower back, shoulders, and chest. You may find it difficult at first, but the other exercises in this circuit will help you attain the needed strength and flexibility to do it.

From a standing position, spread your legs apart to the sides as far as possible. When you feel that you can't lower yourself any farther, lean forward and put your palms (or if you can, your forearms) flat on the floor. Rock from back to front so that you feel a good stretch in your inner thighs. For this exercise you need not keep your feet flat on the floor—you can balance on the sides of your feet or your heels.

S PLIT-PREPARATION A   Hold at least 20 seconds each leg

Kneel on your left leg so that it is bent at a ninety-degree angle and extend your right leg straight out in front of you. Keeping your hips square, bend forward. Your hands can touch the floor on either side of the straight leg for balance or you can grab hold of the leg and pull your upper body down. Switch legs and repeat.

S PLIT-PREPARATION B   **Hold at least 20 seconds each leg**

Kneel on your right leg and put your left leg in front of you with knee bent and foot flat on the floor. Placing your hands on the floor on both sides of your left leg for balance, transfer your weight onto your left foot and straighten your right leg out behind you. Tuck under the toes of your right foot so the top of the foot is resting on the floor, then slide your right foot back as far as you can. Now push your hips toward the floor.

Change legs and repeat.

Splits are not impossible; however, it takes a lot of time and persistence for most people to become this flexible. This move should be attempted only after considerable work with the two preceding split-preparation exercises.

Kneel on your right leg with your left leg extended straight out in front of you. Slide your left leg forward and your right leg back as far as possible. Use your hands on both sides of your left leg for support.
Switch legs and repeat.

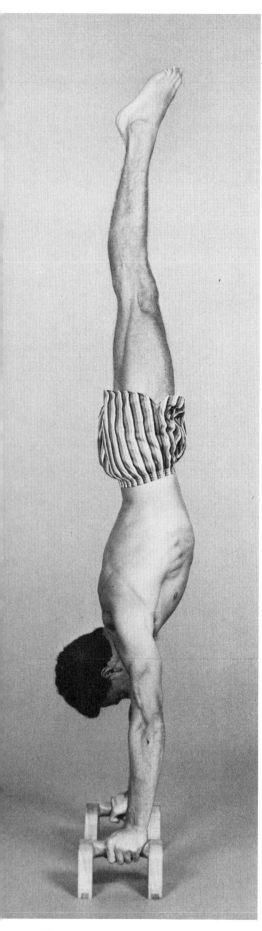

Abdominal Exercises

Good, strong abdominal muscles are an important part of fitness. A gymnast would not be successful in his sport without them. Take the basic move everyone associates with gymnastics—the handstand. It looks best when held in a nice, straight line. Without abdominal strength, the gymnast would find himself in an unattractive arch. Every single move in gymnastics—see Mitch doing a pommel circle opposite—requires complete body control and the stomach is largely responsible for maintaining this. This is true even for good posture in a simple standing position, so abdominal muscles are something everyone should be concerned with. In addition, a strong stomach helps prevent lower-back injuries, and, let's face it, a flat, toned stomach is attractive.

The following exercises will primarily strengthen your abdominal muscles, although you may notice that they work other parts of the body as well. The number of reps suggested as a starting point for each exercise is intended for a person already in reasonably good shape. If you can't do that many initially, don't worry about it. Do what you can and gradually increase. On the other hand, don't be afraid to start with more reps if you can.

The exercises are listed in order of increasing difficulty. If you have weak abdominals and need a lot of work in this area, gradually increase the number of reps in the beginning exercises. As your abdominals become stronger, you'll benefit more by increasing the number of reps in the later exercises. More exercises for your abdominals can be found in the advanced exercise section of the book. Add them to your circuit when you've mastered the exercises in this section. In general, abdominal muscles get little exercise while you're going about your daily business, so it's imperative to give them a good workout when you exercise. The key to developing strong abs is to exercise them *every day,* or close to it.

In all abdominal exercises, make sure to keep your back rounded and your chin down. Do *not* arch your back—this will put too much stress on your lower back and may cause injury.

Chuck Gaylord demonstrating the correct straight line of a handstand

Mitch Gaylord doing a pommel circle

ENT-LEG SIT-UPS, WITH OR WITHOUT ASSISTANCE

Starting number of reps: 15 / Goal: 50

Lie on your back with your knees bent and feet flat on the floor. Fold your arms across your chest and, keeping your chin down, pull yourself up (without jerking) into a sitting position. As you go back down, make sure that your back stays rounded—try to feel your spine roll down to the floor. Don't go all the way down, but keep your shoulders off the floor.

If you need to, anchor your feet under something heavy or have someone hold them. However, you'll get a much better workout if you do these unassisted.

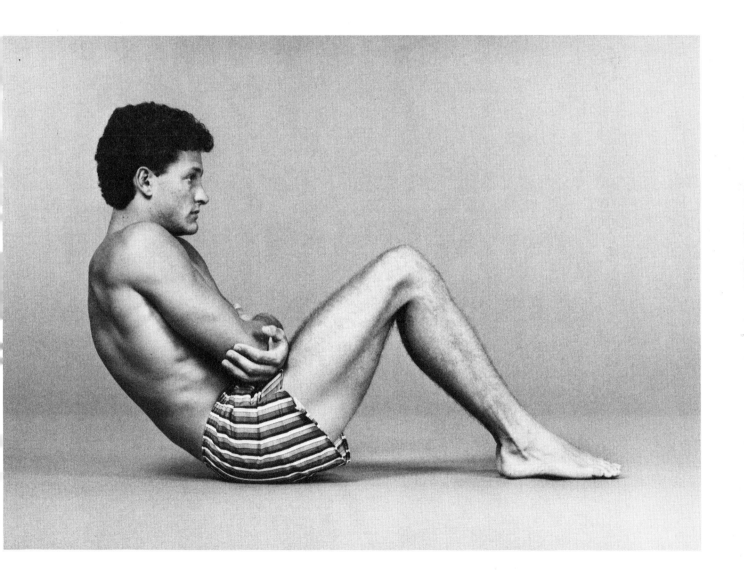

B ODY TIGHTENERS A

Starting number of reps: 2, holding 20 seconds each / Goal: 2, holding 1 minute each

Lie on your back with your feet together and your legs straight. Place your hands on top of your thighs. With your chin down, lift your shoulders and feet four to six inches off the floor. Squeeze your legs together tightly, point your toes, and hold. Don't forget to keep breathing.

Alternate repetitions of this exercise with those of the next.

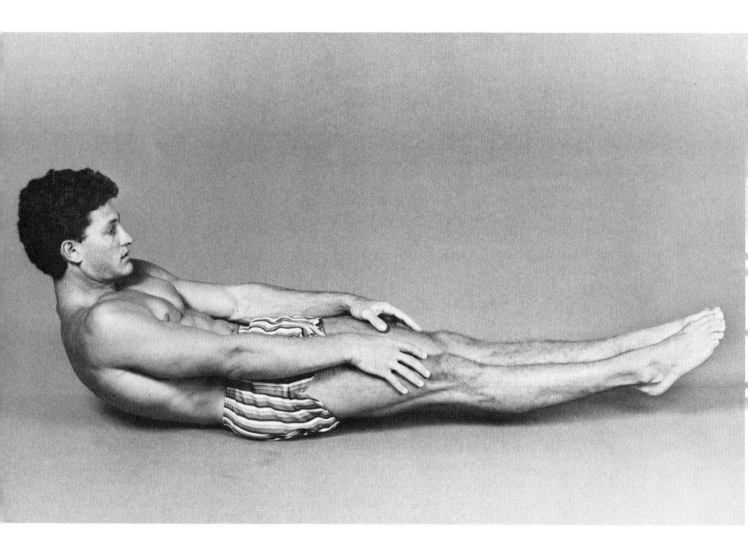

ODY TIGHTENERS B

Starting number of reps: 2, holding 20 seconds each / Goal: 2, holding 1 minute each

Lie on your stomach with your feet together and your legs straight. Place your hands, one on top of the other, under your chin. Lift your upper body so that your elbows and hands are about three inches off the floor; simultaneously lift your feet about four to six inches off the floor, pointing your toes and squeezing your legs together tightly.

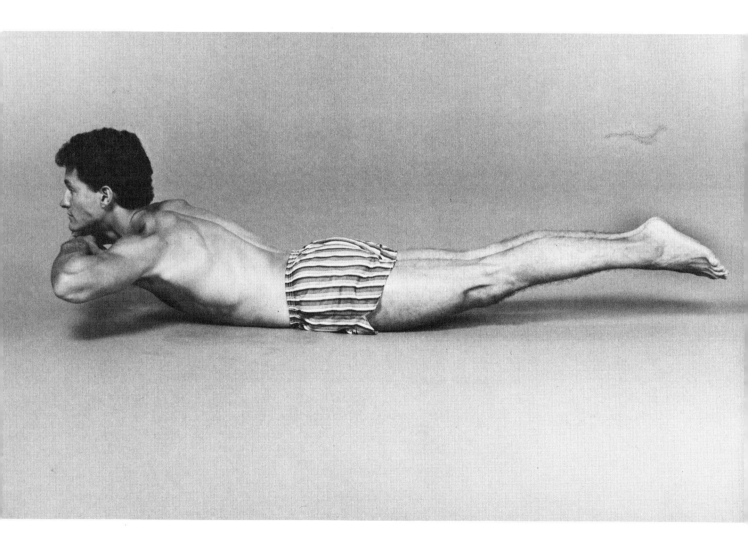

Lie on your back with your legs straight and feet together. Hold your arms at your sides, hands next to your hips, about six inches off the floor. Simultaneously lift your upper body into a sitting position and pull your knees up to your chest so that you're balancing on your buttocks. Immediately after hitting this position, roll your spine back down to the floor and straighten your legs—but don't let your feet or shoulders touch the floor.

ALF–SIT-UP HOLDS, THREE POSITIONS

Starting number of reps: 3 / Goal: 10

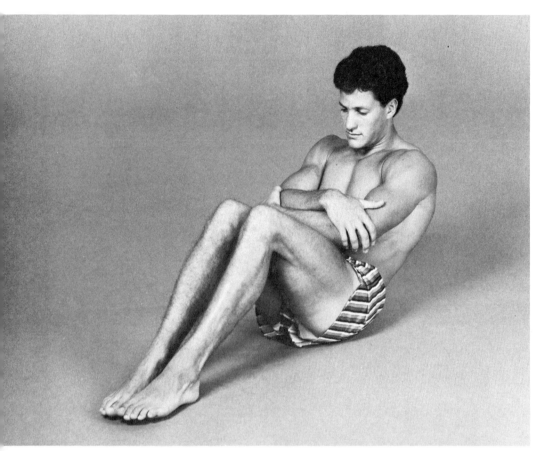

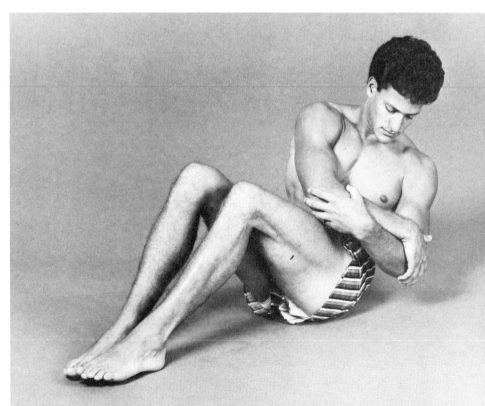

Lie on the floor with your knees bent, feet flat on the floor. Cross your arms over your chest and, keeping your chin down, sit up half the distance between the floor and your knees. Hold for five seconds, then relax and let your spine roll down to the floor to the starting position. Sit up the same distance again, twisting your shoulders slightly to the left. Hold for five seconds and roll down to the starting position. Repeat, twisting your shoulders to the right. Again, hold for five seconds and roll down. This constitutes one repetition.

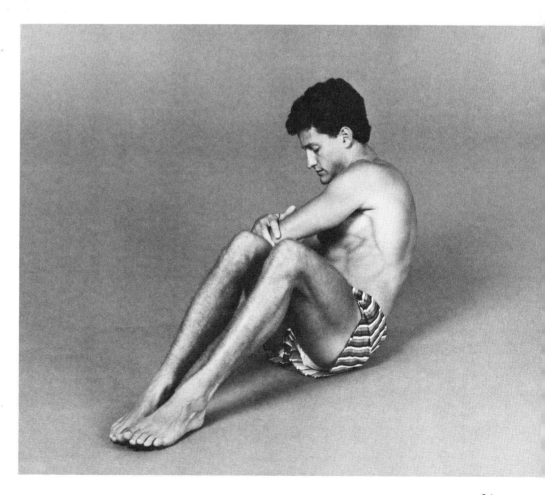

HANGING L'S

Hang from a chinning bar, arms shoulder-width apart, fingers facing forward (this is called an overgrip; fingers facing back is called an undergrip). Keeping your legs straight and toes pointed (if possible—your chinning bar may not be high enough), lift your legs until they are parallel to the floor—so that your legs and body form an "L." Hold for three seconds. Lower and repeat.

An iron cross on rings

A flair on pommel horse

Upper-Body Strength Exercises

Developing strength in the upper body is the primary goal of gymnastics strength exercises. Other athletes work on their feet, but, with the exception of vaulting and floor exercise, the gymnast spends all his time supporting his weight with his arms, shoulders, back, and chest. Chances are you'll never do an iron cross on the rings, a flair on the pommel horse, or a one-arm giant on the high bar. But you will get some idea of what it feels like to support yourself with your upper body when you learn the handstand position.

Again, I've suggested a minimum number of reps as a starting point for each exercise and a goal to work toward. If you can't do the minimum, do as many as you can and try to work your way up. If the minimum isn't challenging enough, start at a higher number of reps.

You'll probably find it difficult to go directly from one exercise to the next in this section, so to relax your muscles, give yourself a breather of a few minutes after each exercise.

A one-arm giant on high bar

SIMPLE PUSH-UPS   *Starting number of reps: 5 / Goal: 15*

Lie on your stomach, with your legs out straight, feet flexed, hands flat on the floor next to your shoulders, fingers pointing forward. Push up until your arms straighten completely and your body comes up off the floor as one unit. Immediately go back down until your stomach or chest lightly touches the floor. As you go down your elbows should bend back, so that they stay directly by your sides.

If you've got parallettes, use them instead of the floor here (and on all following push-up exercises). They enable you to go through a greater range of motion. With parallettes, your fingers will be pointing outward, away from your body, not forward, as directed above. Also, depending on the height of your parallettes, you may not be able to touch your chest to the floor, so go down as far as you can comfortably.

Push-ups are a simple exercise that everyone knows, but here are some things to remember for this and the following exercises:

- Your buttocks and legs should be tightly squeezed together
- Don't sag at the waist
- Keep your back rounded; don't let your chest sag
- Don't jackknife your hips so that they are higher than the rest of your body

Technique is the most important thing. It's more beneficial (and much harder) to do fewer push-ups correctly than to do more with improper technique.

One of the great advantages of push-ups is that they work a variety of muscle groups. However, by varying slightly the way in which you perform push-ups, you can use them to focus somewhat on specific muscles. The simple push-up that you just learned, for example, is particularly good for anterior deltoids. In the following pages you'll learn several more versions of the push-up, each of which, in addition to the overall benefits, emphasizes certain muscles.

Simple push-up, side view

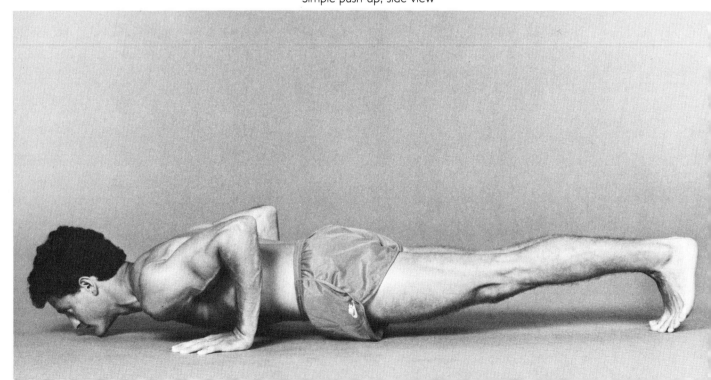

Simple push-up, on parallettes

PUSH-UPS WITH ELBOWS BENDING OUTWARD

Starting number of reps: 5 / Goal: 15

Perform in the same manner as the simple push-up, remembering all the points of good technique, but in this version the elbows bend out, away from the body. I want to stress again that your back should be rounded and your body tight.

This exercise is particularly good for your triceps.

USH-UPS WITH ELBOWS BENDING OUTWARD

Starting number of reps: 5 / Goal: 15

Push-up with elbows bending outward, on parallettes

WIDE-ARM PUSH-UPS

Starting number of reps: 5 / Goal: 15

Move each hand out six inches farther than shoulder width, and do push-ups with elbows bending out. These especially benefit your pectorals.

Wide-arm push-up, on parallettes

With fingers facing forward, put your hands together under the center of your chest so that the thumbs are side by side. Do push-ups with elbows bending backward, alongside your body. These are good for your pectorals and triceps.

Push-up with hands together, on parallettes

If you're using parallettes, put them as close together as possible under the center of your chest, and, of course, your fingers will be pointing outward.

R EVERSE PUSH-UPS **Starting number of reps: 5 / Goal: 15**

Sit with your legs straight out in front of you and place your hands on the
floor, fingers facing away from your body, slightly behind your shoulders.
Slide your feet out as far as you can, so that your buttocks lift off the floor,
your body straightens, and you're supporting your weight with your hands
and your heels. Now, squeezing your legs and buttocks together and
trying to keep your body as straight as possible—there will be some bend

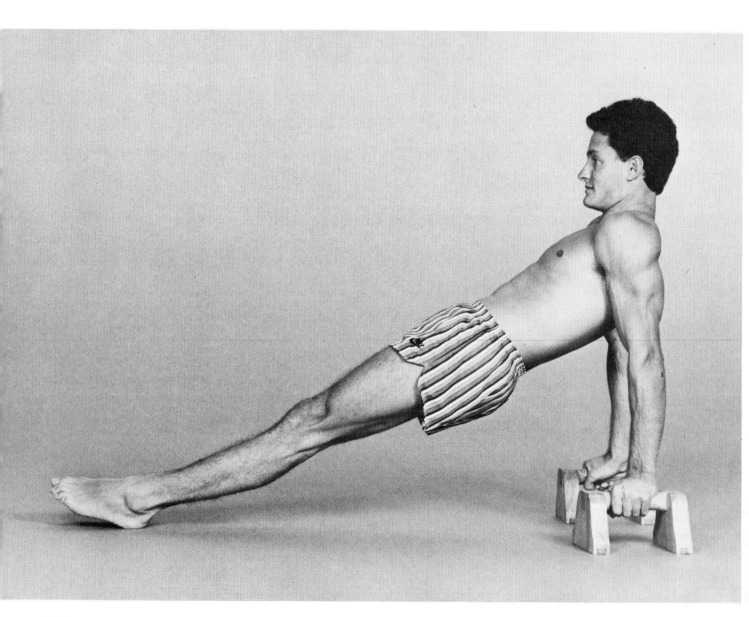

at the waist, but try to keep it to a minimum—lower your body as far as you can (ideally so that your arms bend at least ninety degrees) and then immediately push yourself back up until your arms are straight again. The main thing here is not to let your hips sag too much as you go down. Reverse push-ups work your triceps and lats.

This exercise, in particular, is more beneficial when done on parallettes.

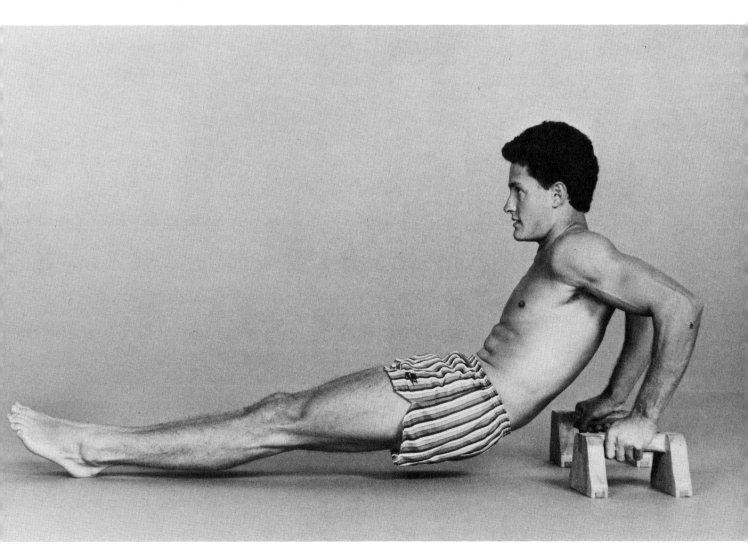

O VERGRIP PULL-UPS

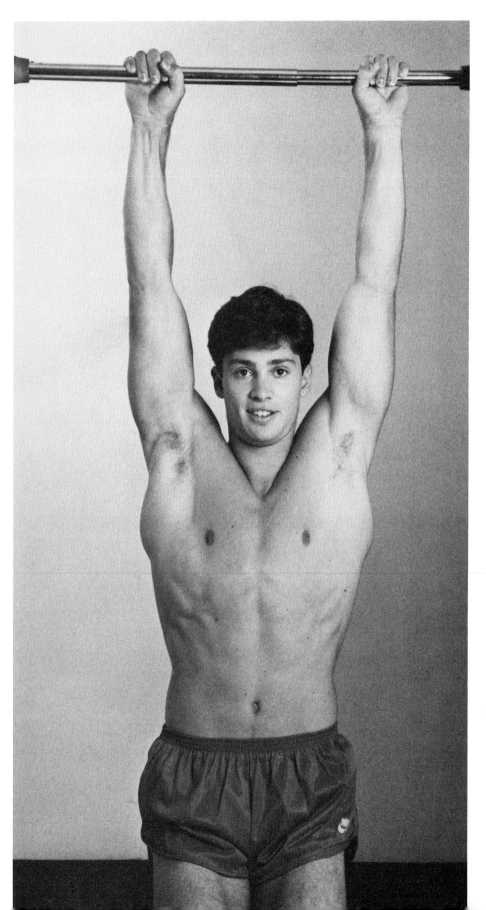

Grab the bar with an overgrip (fingers facing forward), hands shoulder-width apart. From a relaxed, hanging position, pull your body up until your chin clears the top of the bar. Immediately come down again until your arms are completely straight. Overgrip pull-ups are good for your upper back, lats, and forearms.

If possible, hang your chinning bar high enough so that you can do these with straight legs; then make sure to squeeze your legs and buttocks together and point your toes.

If you don't have the strength yet to do a pull-up, hang your bar low enough so that you can bend your knees and hang with your chin above the bar, arms fully bent in an undergrip (fingers facing toward you). Hang in this position as long as you can.

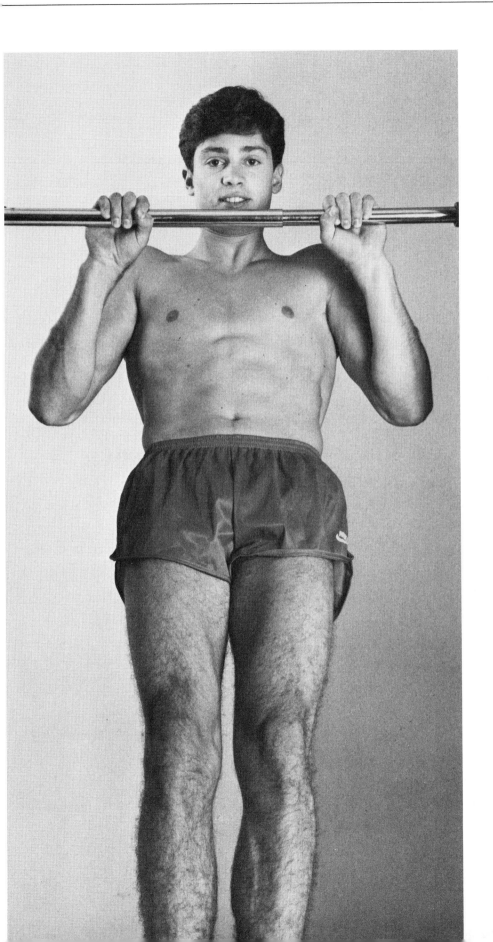

This is essentially the same exercise as the preceding one, except that the bar is gripped with fingers facing toward you. Again,

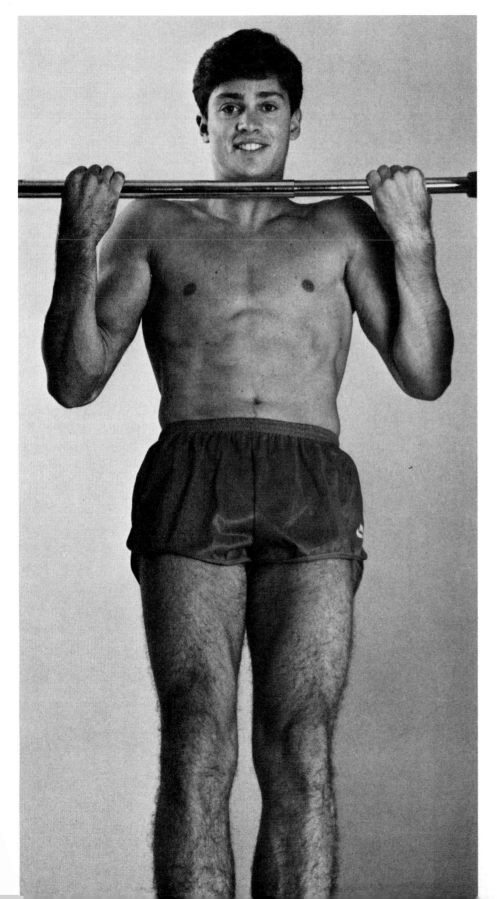

remember to completely straighten your arms at the bottom. Undergrip pull-ups work your biceps especially hard.

Leg Exercises

While gymnastics stresses upper-body strength, the legs cannot be neglected. Gymnasts must have quick, powerful legs for tumbling and vaulting, and for landing from as high as fifteen feet (in high-bar dismounts).

To withstand the demands that their sport places on their legs, gymnasts have developed special exercises. You've already been introduced to one of these in the warm-up section—the punch jump. Here are a couple more. Wear sneakers for the exercises in this section.

High-bar dismounts can require landings from as high as fifteen feet.

T OE RAISES

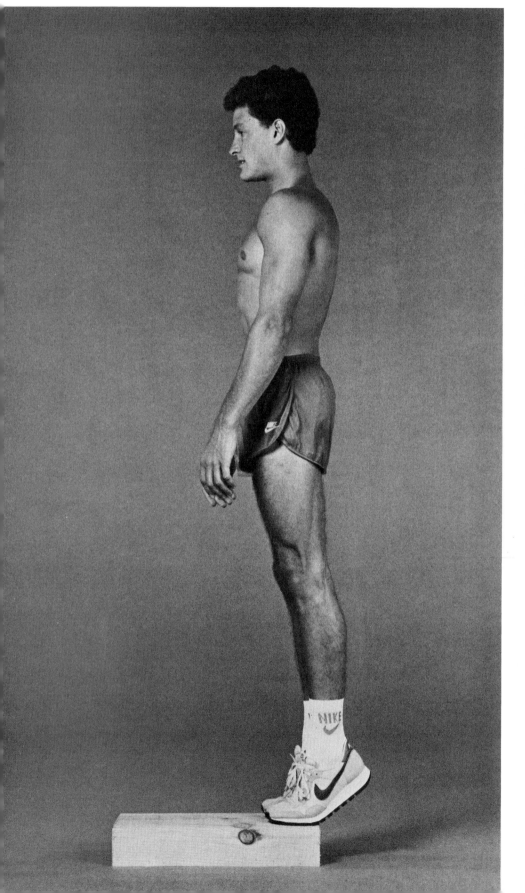

Stand with your feet together and flat on the floor. Rise onto your toes as high as you can, and then return your heels slowly to the floor.

This exercise is far more effective if you put the balls of your feet on a raised surface (such as the edge of a stair or a 2 × 4) so that when you come down, your

heels can descend lower than the balls of your feet. You should do enough of these so that you feel a "burn" in your calves and shins.

As you get stronger you may want to try toe raises one leg at a time. In that case, stand on your left leg with your right foot resting against your left calf, then begin. Change legs and repeat.

S QUAT JUMPS

Starting number of reps: 15 / Goal: 25

Standing with your feet shoulder-width apart and your hands at your sides, squat down quickly with straight back until your knuckles scrape the floor at your sides. Then, throwing your arms up into the air, push off on your feet, springing up with all your might, as high as possible. Land with legs slightly bent, your weight on the balls of your feet, not on your heels or toes. Hold for one second and repeat.

ADVANCED EXERCISES

In this section you will find exercises to add to the basic exercise circuit. You should use them when you have reached close to the maximum number of reps for each exercise in the basic circuit and need a further challenge.

The exercises in this section vary in difficulty. The first three are exercises for your abdominal muscles.

The wide-arm hold and wide-arm pull-ups are basically for upper-body strength, although the former also works your abs. The supported L is another abdominal exercise. Gymnasts often use this position in their competitive routines on the rings and parallel bars.

The handstand is one of the basic moves of gymnastics—it can be seen in some form in each of the six events. It's an excellent exercise to develop upper-body strength and overall body tightness. While learning it, I recommend that you work with a partner.

You'll see gymnasts push-up or press-up to a handstand in their routines on floor, rings, and parallel bars. These exercises take a little more time to learn, so don't be discouraged if you can't do

The handstand is one of the basic moves of gymnastics.

them the first time you try. Once you master these moves, however, you'll find them a fun way to build upper-body strength.

The straddle L and the V support are also more difficult exercises, but once you're ready to add them to your circuit, be persistent. At first you may be able to hold each position for only half a second. But if you practice every time you work out, you'll be able to hold them longer and longer. They're excellent for building overall strength and tightness. You'll see gymnasts performing these moves on floor exercise, rings, and parallel bars.

Supported L on the rings

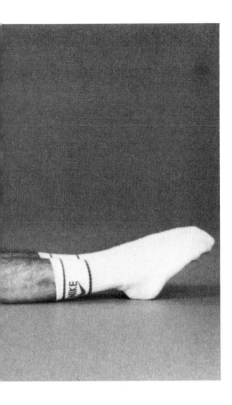

This is an exercise for your abdominal muscles. Lie on your back with your legs straight and together and your arms on the floor, straight out over your head. Leading with your arms, simultaneously raise your upper body and legs, while bending at the hips. Remember to keep your legs straight and your chin down. Touch your toes or as far down your legs as you can. Slowly return to the starting position and repeat. It's important to keep your back rounded in this exercise. Coordinate your upper and lower body so that they rise and fall at the same time.

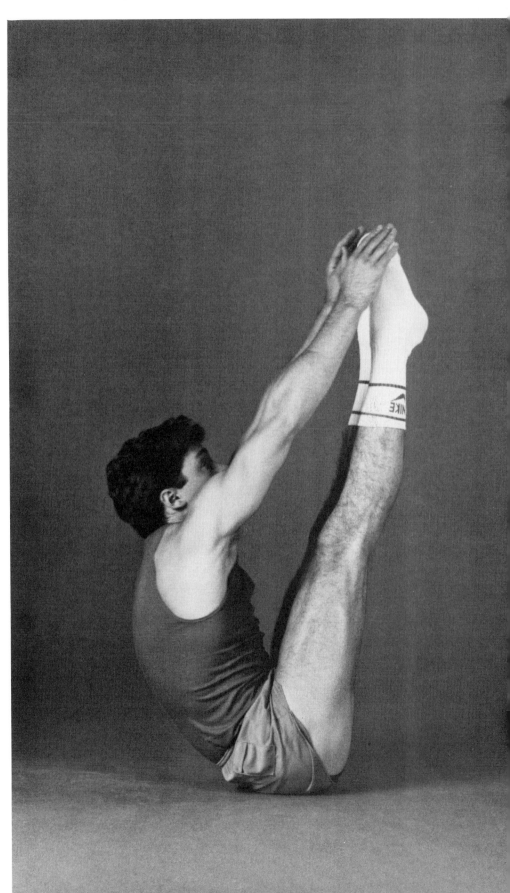

You'll need a partner or something solid to hang on to for this exercise. Lie flat on your back with your legs straight and your arms on the floor straight over your head. Have your partner stand behind you so that you can grab the outside of his ankles, which should be about your shoulder width apart. Keep your legs straight and tightly squeezed together and your toes pointed. Now tuck your hips and raise your body off the floor until your legs are perpendicular to the floor and you're resting on your shoulders. Keeping your back rounded, but without bending too much at the waist, slowly (the slower the better) roll down your spine to the starting position. Remember to keep your chin down, hips tucked under, and your legs and buttocks squeezed tightly together.

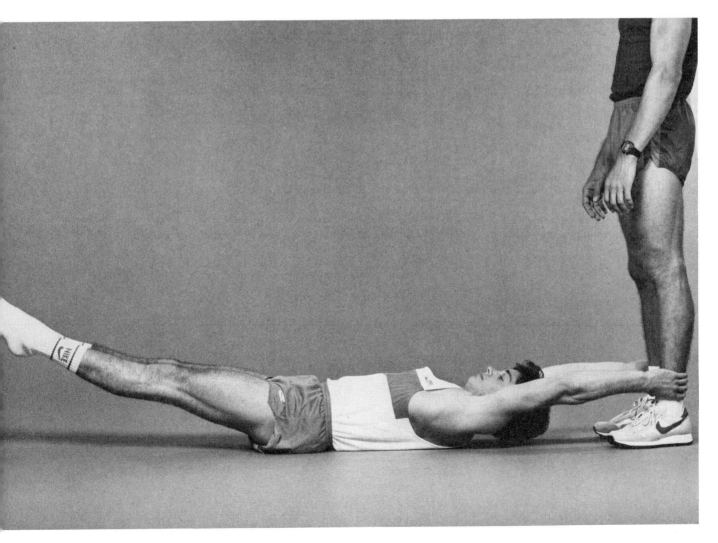

REVERSE BODY LIFTS   **Starting number of reps: 5 / Goal: 25**

This time lie on your stomach with your legs straight and together and your arms straight over your head, on the floor. Have your partner stand in front of you so that you can grip his ankles. Squeezing your legs and buttocks together tightly and keeping your shoulders down, pull with

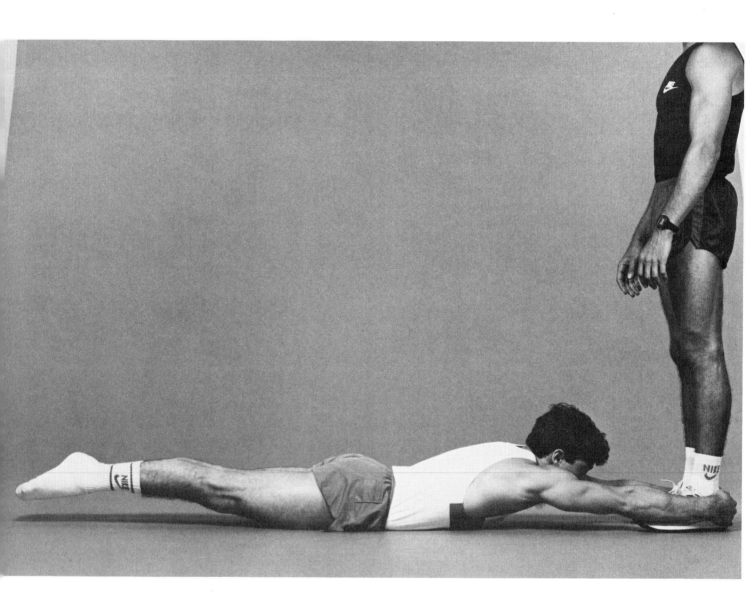

straight arms and rock forward on your chest to raise your legs and hips as far off the floor as you can.

This exercise is basically for your lower back. If you have lower back problems, or find this exercise painful, omit it.

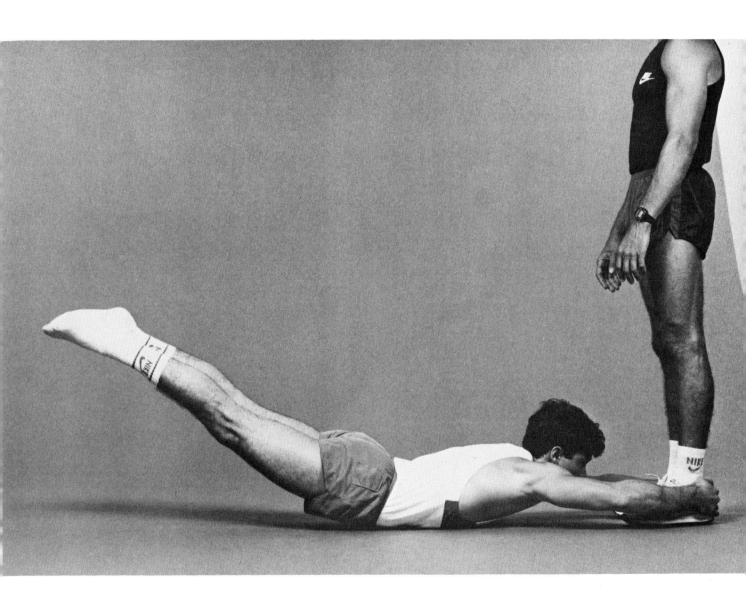

Start in the up position of a push-up, but with your fingers facing outward, away from your body. Slide your hands out as far as possible, until your arms are straight and your chest is only an inch or two off the floor. Hold. Remember to keep your back and chest rounded and your legs and buttocks tightly squeezed together.

This exercise makes your lats and upper chest work harder than they do in regular pull-ups. Using an overgrip on the chinning bar, slide each hand out six inches farther than shoulder width. If your chinning bar is in a doorway, your hands should be touching the sides of the door sill. With your chin

down and head forward, pull up until the back of your neck clears the bar. Then lower slowly until your arms straighten completely. If your chinning bar is high enough, keep your legs straight, legs and buttocks squeezed together, and toes pointed.

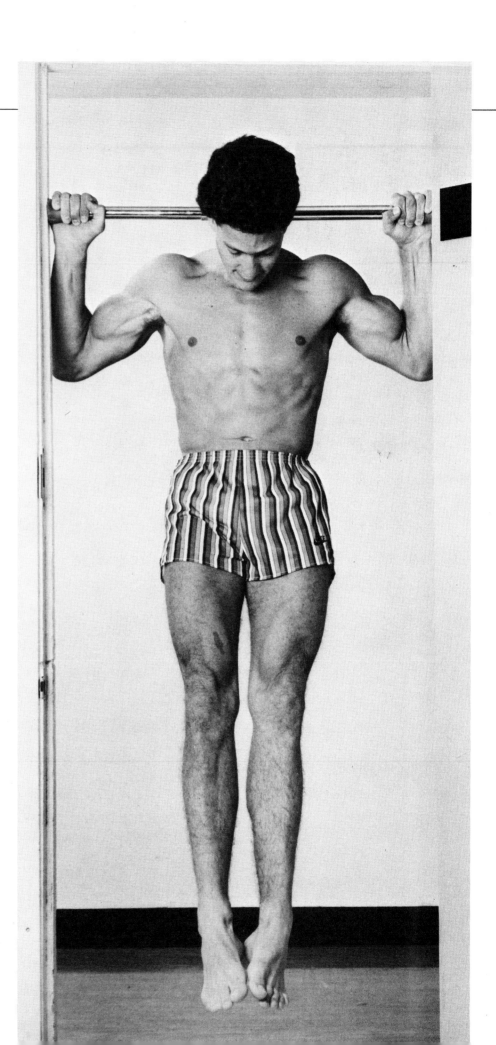

This is primarily an exercise for your abdominal muscles. It's also one of the basic positions used in gymnastics routines on the parallel bars and rings. Most people find this move much easier to do on parallettes than on the floor. Sit with your legs straight out in front of you and put your hands flat on the floor next to your upper thighs (*not* your hips), fingers facing forward. (Or grip the parallettes [which should be shoulder width apart] next to your upper thighs, with fingers facing outward.) Squeeze your legs and point your toes. Now, push down hard until your arms completely straighten and elbows lock, and lift your hips, legs, and feet off the floor, straight out in front of you. Your body should form an "L." Remember to keep your chin up and toes pointed.

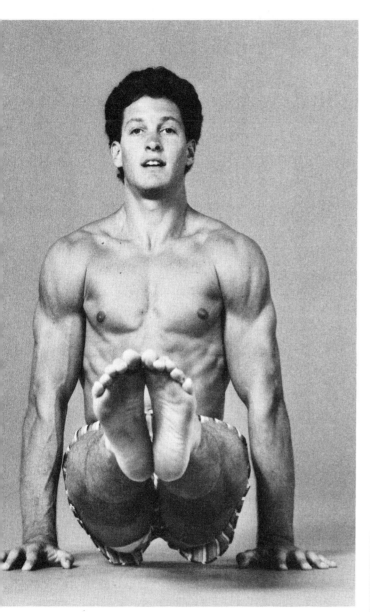

H ANDSTAND

Some people may initially be afraid to try a handstand. It's not really that difficult a move. I taught an exercise class made up of people in their mid-thirties to mid-forties and all of them learned to do one on the first night.

To start off you should use a

wall and a partner. Face the wall
on all fours with your palms
shoulder-width apart, about eight
to ten inches from the wall. Pull
one knee up to your chest and put
that foot on the floor, then extend
the other leg straight behind you,
so that that foot also rests on the
floor. You're in a position now not
unlike a runner starting a race, but
your hips are higher.

Keeping your arms straight and
elbows locked, *look between your
hands,* push off with the front foot
and kick off with the rear leg until
both legs join together over your
head in a handstand. At this point
you may want to rest your feet
against the wall for balance. Have a
partner assist you the first few
times you try this. As you kick up,
he should grab you firmly at the
knees, lifting slightly and steadying
you until you are balanced.

While in the handstand,
remember that your arms should
be completely straight, elbows
locked, and your buttocks and legs
squeezed together tightly. Try not
to arch your back.

When you want to come down,
do it one leg at a time. Initially,
have your partner support you by
placing one hand under your
stomach. As you begin to feel
more confident, try not to touch
your feet against the wall, using
your stomach to maintain a straight
line. When you feel certain you can
balance on your own, try it without
the wall.

If you have parallettes, use them
for the handstand; you may find it
easier to balance with them.

129

H ANDSTAND PUSH-UPS

This is an exercise highly valued by gymnasts. It's an excellent way to increase your overall upper-body strength, and especially good for triceps and deltoids.

Handstand push-ups should be attempted only after you have mastered the handstand. Always use a partner or a wall to help you balance.

From a handstand position, lower yourself so that your legs are straight over your head and your arms bend as far as possible (but can still get you back up), ideally to at least ninety degrees. Immediately push back up into a handstand. Remember to keep your legs and buttocks tightly squeezed together and your toes pointed throughout this exercise. Don't arch your back.

This is a difficult exercise and it may take you awhile to learn it. Only attempt it with a partner, and after you've mastered the handstand.

Stand with your feet a little farther than shoulder width apart. Place your palms flat on the floor, fingers facing forward, about shoulder width apart and six inches from the front of your feet. Your knees should not be bent

this point. Slowly transfer your weight to your arms, lifting your heels off the floor and going up on your toes. Push down hard on your arms, raising your hips over your head, so that your legs are in a wide straddle in the air. Now bring your legs up and together into a handstand position. This entire exercise should be done in one slow, fluid movement.

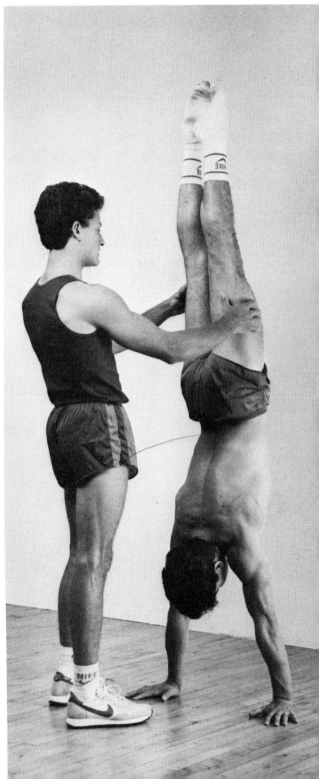

Starting point: Hold 3 seconds / Goal: Hold 20 seconds

The straddle L is a move you'll see in competitive gymnastics. It's extremely good for your abdominals and upper legs. Like the supported L, this exercise is possible from the floor, but easier on parallettes.

Sit with your legs straight and as far apart as possible. Place your hands flat on the floor, fingers facing forward, between your legs, as close as possible to your upper thighs and shoulder width apart (or grip the parallettes in the same position). Push down hard until your arms straighten, lifting your hips, legs, and feet off the floor. Try to keep your chin up, legs straight, and toes pointed.

This is a difficult exercise. However, doing the other exercises in this book will eventually supply you with the strength necessary to do it. Like the supported L and the straddle L, it is easier on parallettes.

From a supported L position, lift your legs up as high as you can, so that your body forms a tight "V."

EXERCISES FOR THE GYM

After doing the exercises in this book, you may find that you want to get up on some real gymnastics equipment. Check out your local gymnasiums—many have at least a set of parallel bars. Look for one that has rings and a high bar as well. For your first few times, you should find someone who's familiar with the apparatus to spot you. Always make sure there are mats underneath you. To keep your hands from getting slippery, put chalk on them before exercising.

Should you decide you really want to pursue gymnastics seriously, inquire at the gym about gymnastics classes. You can also write to the United States Gymnastics Federation, Merchants' Plaza, Suite 1144e, 101 West Washington St., Indianapolis, Indiana 46204 to find out about gymnastics clubs in your area.

MUSCLE-UP ON THE RINGS   **Starting number of reps: 1 / Goal: 5**

For this exercise the rings have to be gripped in a special way: You overgrip them so the rings run through your palms and rest on the inside of your wrists. Gymnasts call this a false grip. Now, keeping the rings a little closer than shoulder width apart, do a pull-up until your shoulders are level with the rings. Rock forward and point your elbows up so that you're supporting yourself *on* your hands. Now push up and straighten your arms, keeping your hands close to your sides. This finishing position i called a support.

    To get down reverse the process.

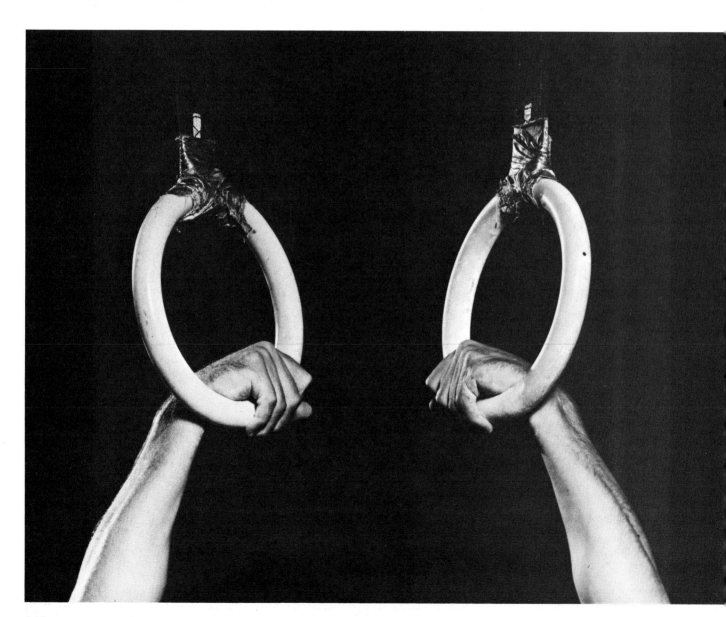

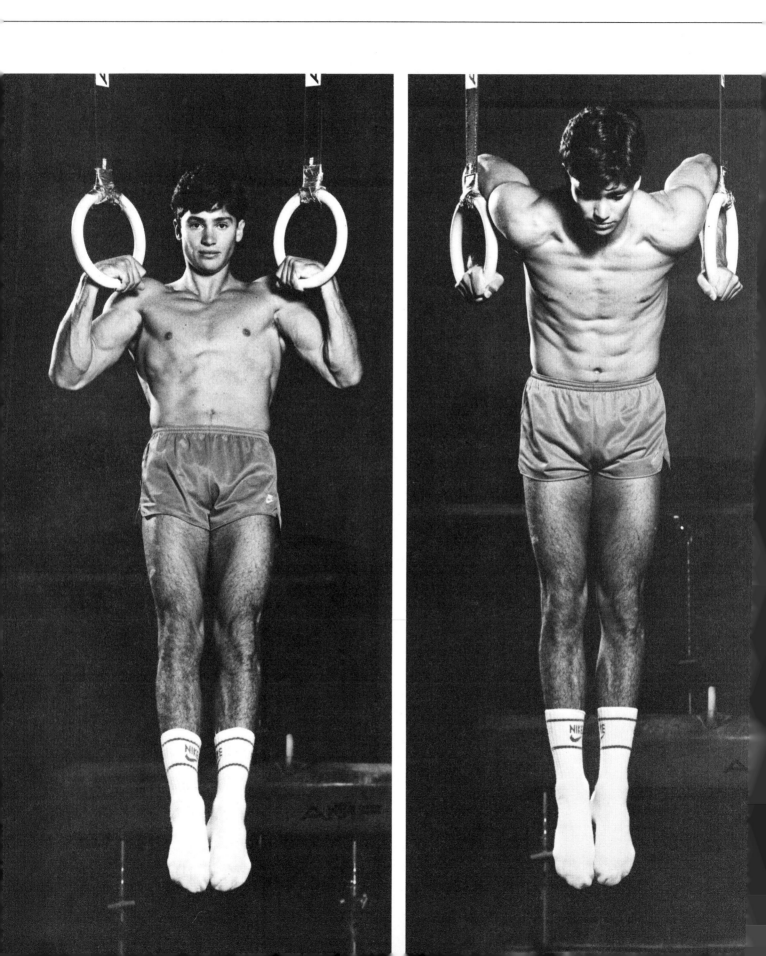

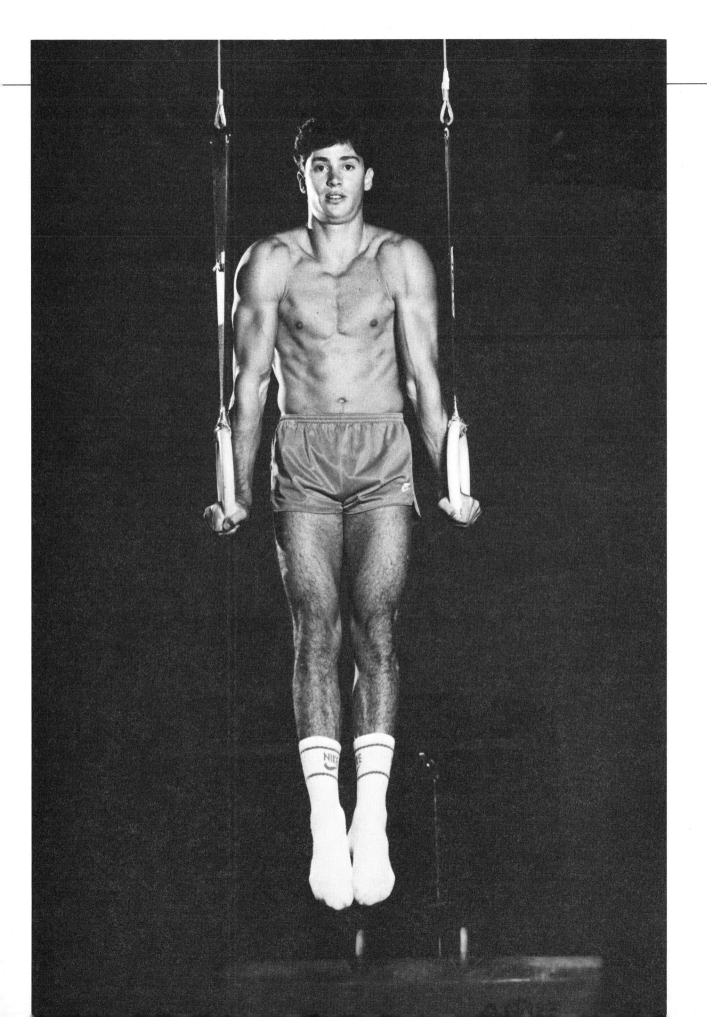

Hold a support position above the rings (the finishing position of a muscle up, with your arms straight and the rings close by the sides of your legs). If your rings are low enough, you don't have to do a muscle-up to get there. Simply jump up into the position. Squeeze your hips and legs together and point your toes. Your legs should be hanging straight down below you.

We've already illustrated the supported L position on the floor, parallettes, and chinning bar. On the rings, however, this position is a little more difficult, because you have to hold the rings steady by your sides.

From a support position, lift your legs into an L and hold.

Grab the bar in an overgrip, hands shoulder width apart, body completely extended. Keeping your legs straight and together with toes pointed, lift your legs past the hanging L position until your feet lightly touch the bar. Lower your legs slowly to the starting position and repeat.

FRONT-LEVER PULL-UPS ON HIGH BAR

Starting number of reps: 3 / Goal: 15

Grab the bar in an overgrip, hands shoulder width apart. Keeping your legs and buttocks squeezed tightly together and toes pointed, pull yourself up to a full pull-up position. Without bending at the hips, rock back and simultaneously lift your legs, drop back your shoulders and straighten your arms. At this point your body should be parallel to the floor with your hands directly over your chest. Immediately pull your arms in and drop your legs so that you end back in the up position of a pull-up.

S IMPLE DIPS ON THE PARALLEL BARS   **Starting number of reps: 3 / Goal: I**

Jump up to a support position on the parallel bars—if your bars are too high, find something safe to stand on so that you can jump up. In a support position here, you should be between the bars, one hand on each bar, arms completely straight with your legs hanging straight below you.

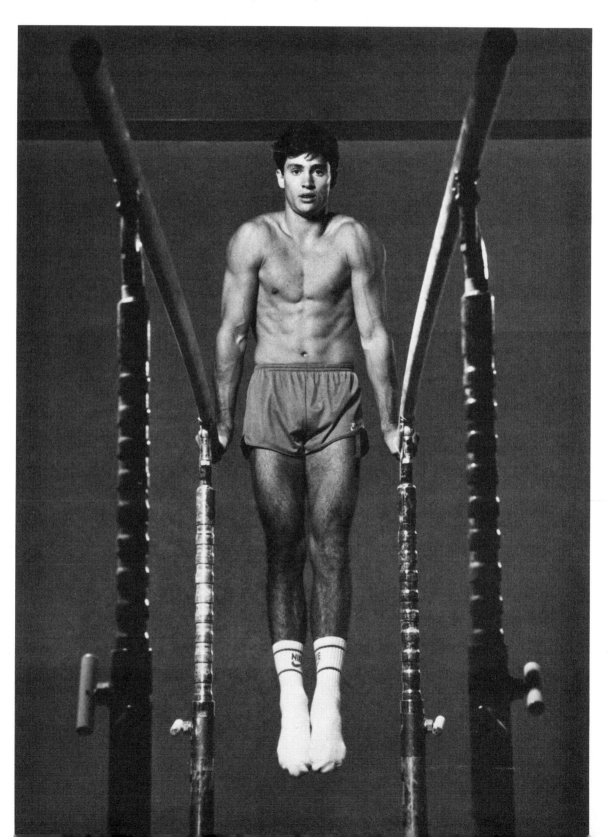

Lower yourself until your arms bend past ninety degrees, then slowly push back up to a support position. Dips are good for your deltoids, pectorals, and triceps.

PPER-ARM-REST DIPS ON THE PARALLEL BARS

Starting number of reps: 5 / Goal: 20

Stand between the bars, but instead of jumping up in a support position, grab the outside of the bars so that your upper arms are resting on top of the bars and supporting your weight. Let your shoulders dip below the level of the bars, then pull down with your elbows so that your shoulders rise as far above the bars as possible.

This exercise is especially good for your lats and pectorals. The higher you can get your shoulders in the top position, the greater the benefit you'll derive.

UPPORT SWINGS ON THE PARALLEL BARS

Starting number of reps: 2 / Goal: 15

From a straight-arm support position, squeeze your legs and buttocks together and point your toes. Now, without bending at the waist, swing your body as high up as you can in front of you. Then let yourself drop and swing as high up as you can in back. Use your stomach to control the height of the swing.

When you first do this exercise, start with small swings. As you build confidence, you'll be able to swing higher and higher.

INDEX

A

abdominal exercises
    bent-leg sit-ups, with or without
        assistance, 74–75
    body tighteners A, 76
    body tighteners B, 77
    half–sit-up holds, three positions,
        80–81
    hanging L's, 82–84
    tuck-ups, 78–79
advanced exercises
    body lifts, 118–19
    handstand, 128–29
    handstand push-ups, 130–31
    press to a handstand, 132–33
    reverse body lifts, 120–21
    supported L's, 126–27
    straddle L, 134–35
    V support, 136–37
    V-ups, 116–17

B

back bend, 64–65
basic exercise circuit, 17, 19
    advantage of, 19
    exercises in
        abdominal exercises, 72
        leg exercises, 107
        stretching, 33
        upper-body strength exercises, 85
        warm-ups, 23
bent-leg sit-ups, with or without
        assistance, 74–75
body lifts, 118–19
body tighteners A, 76
body tighteners B, 77

C

calf and Achilles tendon stretches, 49
cross-arm swings, 38–39

D

diet, importance of, 18
dips
    simple, on parallel bars, 154–55
    upper-arm-rest, on parallel bars,
        152–53

E

exercises for the gym, 17
    front-lever pull-ups on high bar,
        150–51
    leg lifts on high bar, 148–49
    L support on rings, 146–47
    simple dips on parallel bars, 152–53
    support hold on rings, 144–45
    support swings on parallel bars, 156–57

F

forward and backward arm circles, 36–37
front-lever pull-ups on high bar, 150–51

G

gymnastics
    advantages of, 13, 19, 22
    disadvantages of, 18
    equipment for, 14, 17, 19, 20, 21, 139
    as fitness program, 10
    outmoded scoring in, 9
    rewards of, 9

H

half–sit-up holds, three positions, 80–81
hamstring stretch A, 50–51
hamstring stretch B, 52–53
handstand, 128–29
handstand push-ups, 130–31
hanging L's, 82–84
hopping on one foot, 27

I

inner-thigh stretch, 58–59

J

jumping jacks, 28–29
jumping up and down, 26

L

leg exercises
    squat jumps, 110–12
    toe raises, 108–9
leg lifts on high bar, 148–49
light jog, 25
L support on rings, 146–47

M

muscle-up on rings, 144–45

N

neck rolls, 34–35

O

overgrip push-ups, 102–3

P

parallettes, 20–21
pull-ups
    front-lever, on high bar, 150–51
    undergrip, 104–5
punch jumps, 31–32
push-ups
    with elbows bending outward, 90–93
    handstand, 130–31
    with hands together, 96–99
    overgrip, 102–3
    reverse, 100–101
    simple, 86–89
    wide-arm, 94–95

R

rep, definition of, 17
reverse body lifts, 120–21
reverse push-ups, 100–101

S

shoulder stretch, 60–61
side stretch, 43
simple dips on parallel bars, 152–53
simple push-ups, 86–89
split jumps, 30
split preparation A, 68
split preparation B, 69
splits, 70–71
squat jumps, 110–12
straddle L, 134–35
stretches (-ing), 17
    advantages of, 17, 33
    back bend, 64–65
    calf and Achilles tendon, 49
    cross-arm swings, 38–39
    forward and backward arm circles,
        36–37
    hamstring stretch A, 50–51
    hamstring stretch B, 52–53
    inner-thigh stretch, 58–59

    neck rolls, 34–35
    shoulder stretch, 60–61
    side stretch, 43
    split preparation A, 68
    split preparation B, 69
    splits, 70–71
    stomach and lower-back stretch, 62–6?
    straddle splits, 66–67
    straddle stretch, 54–57
    trunk twisters, 42
    vertical arm swings, 40–41
    wrist stretches, 46–48
supported L's, 126–27
support hold on rings, 144–45
support swings on parallel bars, 156–57

U

undergrip pull-ups, 104–5
upper-arm-rest dips on parallel bars,
        154–55
upper-body strength exercises
    overgrip push-ups, 102–3
    push-ups with elbows bending outward
        90–93
    push-ups with hands together, 96–99
    reverse push-ups, 100–101
    simple push-ups, 86–89
    undergrip pull-ups, 104–5
    wide-arm push-ups, 94–95

V

vertical arm swings, 40–41
V support, 136–37
V-ups, 116–17

W

warm-ups, 17, 23
    hopping on one foot, 27
    jumping jacks, 28–29
    jumping up and down, 26
    light jog, 25
    punch jumps, 31–32
    split jumps, 30
wide-arm push-ups, 94–95
wrist stretches, 46–48